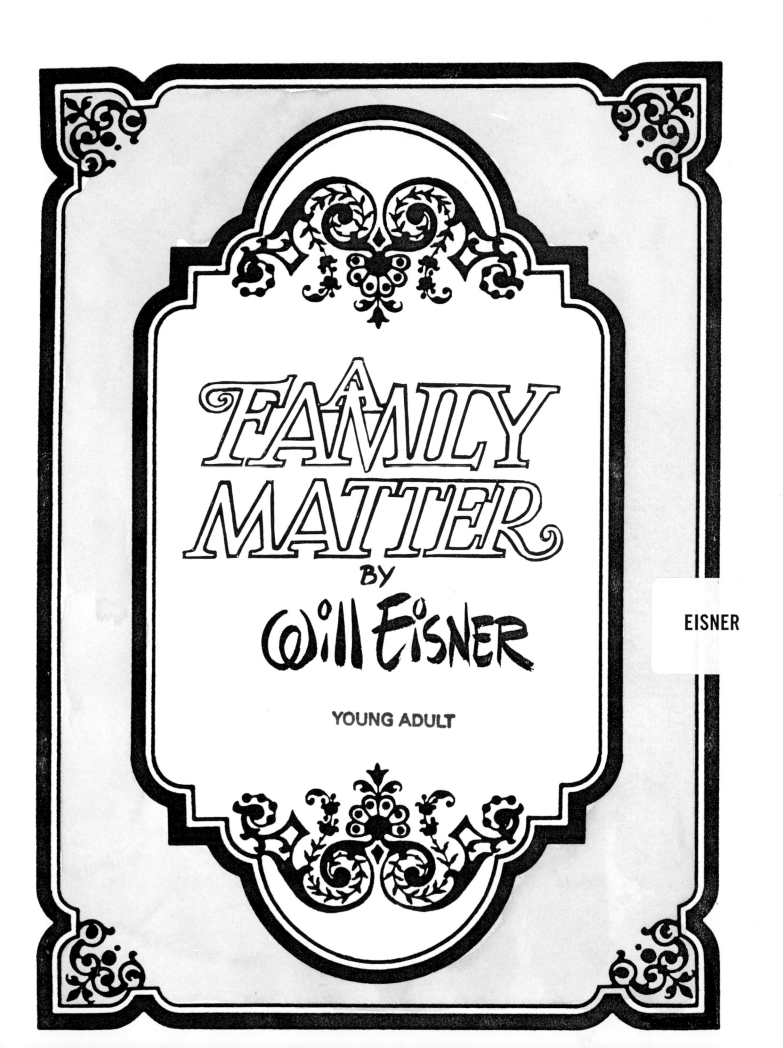

A FAMILY MATTER

BY

Will Eisner

YOUNG ADULT

writer and artist
Will Eisner

publisher
Denis Kitchen

editors
Dave Schreiner, Christopher Couch

art director
C. Evan Metcalf

cover design
Kevin Lison

art intern
Katie Chang

---

vice president
James Kitchen

senior director, sales and marketing
Jamie Riehle

national sales director
Ryan D. Eagan

director of customer service
Karen Lowman

managing editor
John Wills

warehouse manager
Dwight Jackson

Library of Congress Cataloging-in-Publication Data

Eisner, Will.
    A family matter / Will Eisner.
       p. cm.
       ISBN 0-87816-621-1. — ISBN 0-87816-620-3 (softcover)
       I. Title.
       PN6727.E4F36 1998   98-17259
       741.5'973—dc21   CIP

First Printing: July 1998

For a ***FREE*** catalog (mailed in the U.S. only) of Kitchen Sink Press products, including award-winning graphic novel masterpieces by Will Eisner, call 1-800-365-7465, fax 1-413-586-7040, e-mail catalogs@kitchensink.com, or write Kitchen Sink Press, 76 Pleasant Street, Northampton, MA 01060. Visit the KSP Web site and on-line catalog at www.kitchensink.com.

Printed in Spain

THE FAMILY

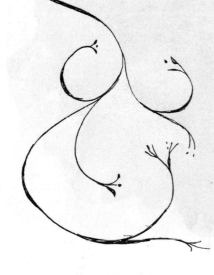

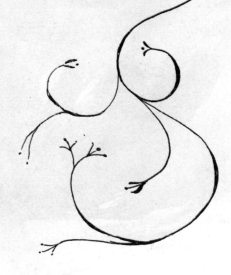

FAMILIES ARE REALLY
PHYSICALLY UNDISTINGUISHABLE
FROM EACH OTHER.
THEY WEAR NO BADGES.
THEY ARE, AFTER ALL,
TRIBAL UNITS
TO WHICH THEIR MEMBERS
BELONG BY VIRTUE OF A
BIOLOGICAL EVENT.
AND
THEY ARE HELD TOGETHER
BY A MAGNETIC CORE THAT
SOMETIMES SEEMS
TO BE NEITHER
LOVE NOR LOYALTY

Anon.

2.

3

4.

6

7.

9

12

15

16

17

18

19

21

23

24

28

29

31

32

34

36

37

38

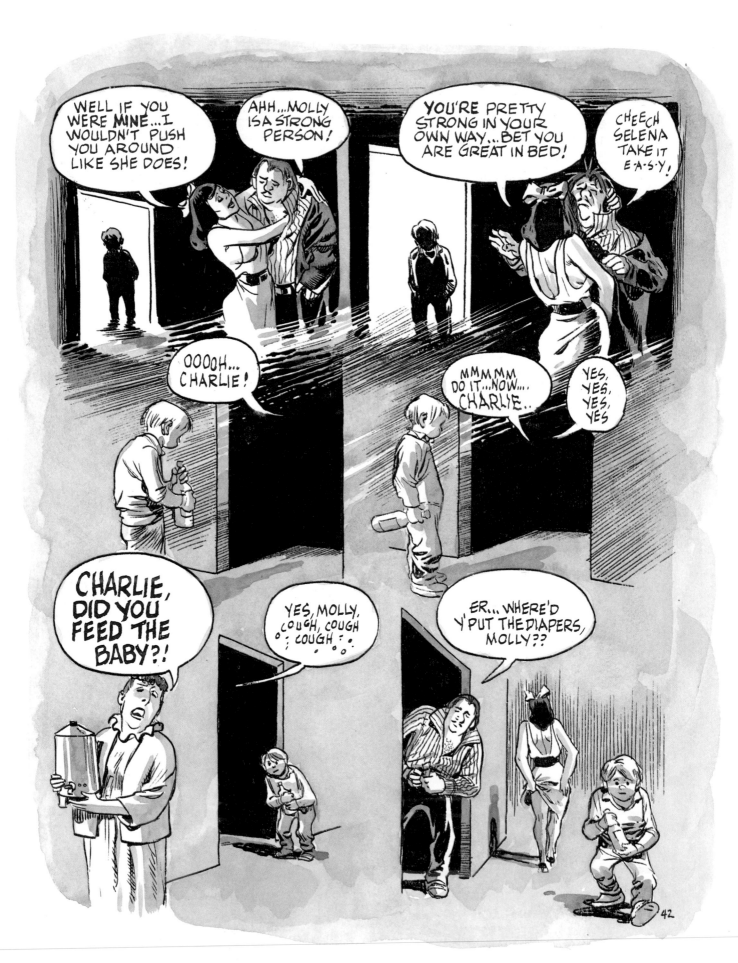

43

45

46

48

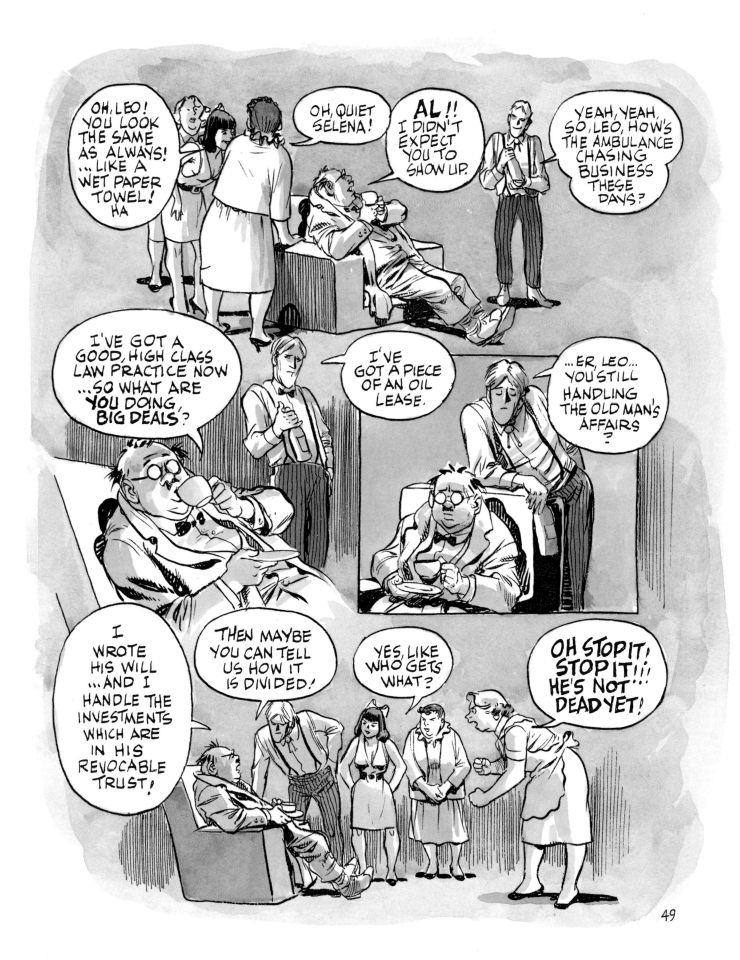

49

50

54

55

61

62

64

65

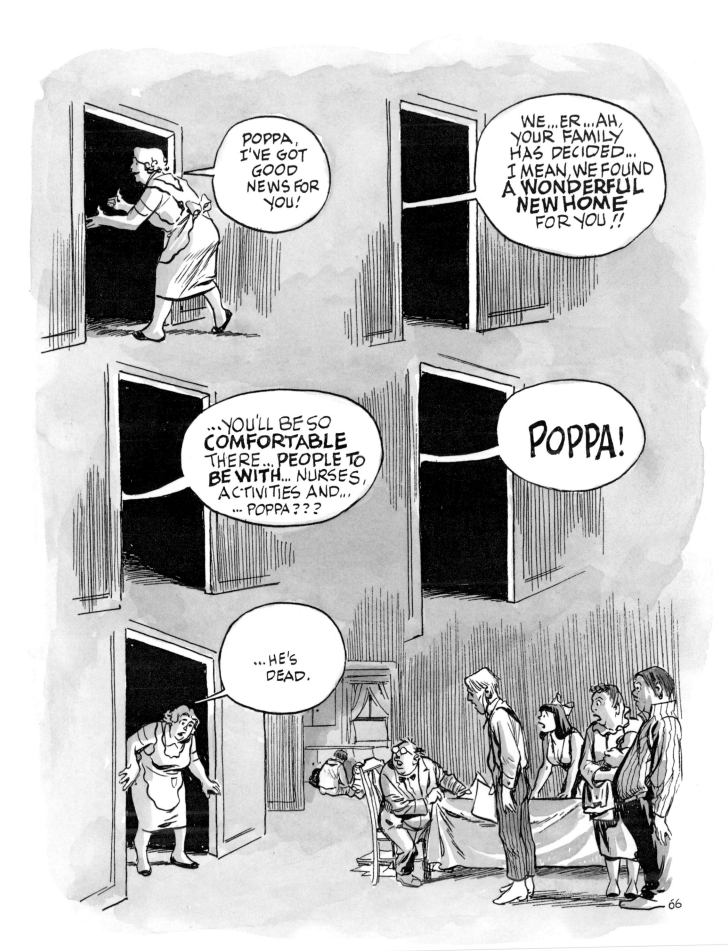